Imagine
Mercy

David Groulx

BookLand
press

Published by BookLand Press
15 Allstate Parkway, Suite 600, Markham, Ontario L3R 5B4
www.booklandpress.com

Printed and bound in Canada.

Library and Archives Canada Cataloguing in Publication

Groulx, David A., 1969-
     Imagine mercy / David Groulx.

(Canadian Aboriginal voices)
Poems.
Issued also in electronic formats.
ISBN 978-1-926956-37-4

     I. Title. II. Series: Canadian Aboriginal voices series

PS8563.R76I43 2013   C811'.54   C2012-908267-8

We acknowledge the support of the Canada Council for the Arts, which last year invested $154 million to bring the arts to Canadians throughout the country. We acknowledge the support of the Ontario Arts Council (OAC), an agency of the Government of Ontario, which last year funded 1,681 individual artists and 1,125 organizations in 216 communities across Ontario for a total of $52.8 million. We acknowledge the financial support of the Ontario Media Development Corporation for our publishing activities.

Table of Contents

Part One

Part Two

Part One

THERE WILL BE LIGHT

War and Rumours of War

There will be war and rumours of war
The poor will rise up and the poor will be beaten
   down again
There will be hope and hope will be lost
There will be promises made and promises broken
There will be war and peace broken
There will be love and there will be hate
There will be peacemakers and evildoers
There will be light and light replaced by dark
This is the way of the world
There will be mercy
Most of all there will be mercy

"He's Native, He Writes Protest Poems"

He writes protest poems
we got the highest rates of incarceration
and short life spans

I ain't got time to write pastoral poems
too busy writing eulogies
we're dying of diabetes, suicide and VD
I ain't got time to write about biocide
and what Rousseau thought
Down here white boy-sex is rape and rape
     is always for sale
if you got the money
and violence is love and love is for sale too
if you wanna pay for it
if you wanna twist it

Busy boiling every drop of water
to make this movie
Protest poems
about stolen sisters
and dead brothers
Protest poems
White boy
White boy
Why do I always get this crazy stuff from you
about what goes on?

I ain't got time to read about it
gonna get my *Guevara*
and my *X*
the cops are always around
and the security guards staring you down
Is it like that in your town?
What do you protest?
NOTHING?

Do you have clean running water?
Does Children's Aid cruise your neighbourhood?
Do the bodies of your sisters keep
turning up in shallow graves
just outside of town?

Just what is it I should write White boy?
pastoral poems about the land
poems about the Confederation Poets
this nation
that nation
this White Boy Nation
has no war bride
it's got widow and orphan
and brown skin
I'M A BROWN BOY
It's got racism and self-hate
It's got overcrowding, corruption and TB

What do you write about White boy?

Protest Poem

I protest the death of Dudley George
I protest the bulldozing of my grandmother's home
I protest the wrongful conviction of Leonard Peltier
I protest the Aboriginal suicide epidemic
I protest clear-cut logging and the destruction of the earth
I protest the turning away of the *St. Louis*
and the *Komagata Maru*
and the "murder" of coal miners
by the RCMP
in Estevan
I protest the power of the Pope
and the ownership of property
and all of John Wayne's movies
I protest the internment of the
Japanese
the Ukrainians
Germans
and Italians
and the deportations
of labour organizers
I protest that *Surfacing* is great literature
and all *Sensitive Men*
I protest the laws against assisted suicide
the idea that capitalists create wealth
and whatever happens on the stock market
I protest the price of gas
the price of bread
and any price paid for in blood

I protest the rapture
original sin
heaven
will
weep
for hell
and transubstantiation
I protest the adversarial legal system
the devil
the lord
and that vengeance is his
I protest that I can make you
do anything
say anything
feel anything
I protest that I
am on my hands and knees now
I protest my brokenness
and your brokenness too
I protest this body
that grows old
this memory that fades
this heart that keeps breaking
and that youth is wasted on
the young
I am on my belly now
I protest death
and I protest wherever we go
when we die
and I protest the darkness

The Same War(s)

I woke up this morning
and the war was on my TV again
the same one that's been on since I was a child
then it was Vietnam in black and white
now Afghanistan/Iraq in colour
war when I was a child
it was us against them
now it is them against us
now I put away my childish things
now let us sing of war
now let us sing of the armless/legless
the gutless
and a reason to be unreasonable
what I knew as a child
I no longer understand
what I remembered as a child
I no longer remember
soon
all I'll remember is war
is war
is war
is war all there is?

If You Listen, If You Say

If it is the other that threatens you
threatens your inhumanity to man
teaches you that Chiquita bananas are good for you
and bad for the rest of the world
that you can be scalped if you go to the Indian reserve
that the war on your TV is the same on
everybody else's
If you win this war, the world loses
If you lose this war, you can hit the reset button
and play it again on Wii
If you speak, you will be heard
but the world will be silent
If you listen, you'll know the world is deaf
If you forget, the world will remember
If you remember, you forget the world
If you speak, I will hear you
If I speak, you will hear the world
If you kill me, you kill the world
If you enslave me, then you can win
and the world loses
If you believe in fate, the world will not believe you
and you will not believe me
If you hate me, then you hate yourself
and if you hate yourself
and you hate the world
hate
and this is all there is to say

Gather on the Bridges

Crowds gather on the bridges
That cross over the highway 401
waving flags and saluting
crying even
as the hearse goes by
His mother is not there
They take pictures with their phones and sing
Oh Canada
Oh Kandahar
another soldier from across the world
they believe the body inside is a hero
dead soldiers always seem to be
inside is only the torso
it was all that was left of him

and tonight and for the rest of her life
his mother will be without a son

What We Never Wanted

I never wanted you to go there
I never wanted you to leave here
I never wanted you to go to a place
I've never heard of
a place I never been to
a place I never will be to/a hell
a place I don't give a fuck about
I never wanted you to murder people
I don't give a damn for
What the hell is this war for?
I don't know how to make you forget
what's in your head
I don't know how to wash the blood from
your hands or mine
You say you did this in my name
I'm to blame because I am silent
silent no more
I never wanted this goddamn war
I never gave a damn about the *Taliban* and *Al-Qaeda*
I never wanted you to come
home like this: *a hearse*
I never wanted you to come home
have a hell living in your head
I never wanted you to come home like this
a puzzle of broken pieces
I could never put back together

Heroes and Survivors

For the soldiers who didn't get killed
you are not heroes
only politicians use that word
to replace dead bodies
with breathing ones
you are not heroes
because you survived
you are survivors

Almost Home from Afghanistan

The townspeople made enough donations
to buy a house with all the ramps and
hallways wide enough for a wheelchair
a local contractor donated his time
to put in the foundation
after he came home from Afghanistan
his arms and legs and all of his dreams
still there
he was twenty-three
it was the least they could do
and this was
the most they could do

Some Are Mistaken

Some people mistake
capitalism for democracy
consumerism for freedom
money for wealth
law for justice
Some people are stupid like this
Some people mistake war for
patriotism
and soldiers for heroes
all heroes are dead.
Some people don't believe there
is power in numbers
but in guns
they are mistaken.
Some people believe
love can save the world
it can
in their belief
love can save the world
they are not mistaken

Water

Here
there is a permanent water advisory
BOIL YOUR WATER
The government calls this progress
ear infections
impetigo
for the children
The government calls this
progress
there is no running water
no taps
no baths
only lake water to wash in the summer time
all Indian children know how to swim
it is a necessity
like clean water

Religious Television

There is a man on my TV
selling holy water
20$ a vial
it will make you rich, *it will saaave yur lifea*
it will maa-ake miracleaza
these things are not miracles
and I already know
water is sacred

Houses up to Attawapiskat

Houses up to Attawapiskat
on the ice roads
which don't last as long as they used to

The prime minister is driving one
of the trucks up himself
because he cares about his Indians
he does it because
he knows how cold it is up there

He hears the wind howling off James Bay
all the way from 22 Sussex
so he drives night and day
won't even stop for a rest
won't even stop for a press conference

He's even run over a moose
just to get there faster
he ties the dead moose on to the cab
of the truck
this will be good for the Indians
he says

How It Is to Be Indian in Canada

You are afraid
conscious that you are not White
you are aware that you are outnumbered
all the time
you feel that you do not belong
But you do
you are always asked stupid questions
like
What's your breed?
What's your Indian name?
What do you do when a coyote passes by?
Do you know so/and/so from Vancouver
or Winnipeg? or Montreal?
When you are Indian in Canada
you know the cops don't normally drive that slow
in Port Arthur or Tuxedo
you know you are a rare commodity for tourists
and easy *pickings* for Children's Aid
your senses are always razor-sharp
on edge
of society
and this makes our lives shorter
and precious

How Canada Was/Is Divided

White people believe Indians
are part of the land
like plants and animals
flora and fauna
They created game reserves for animals
reserves for Indians
and parks for themselves
They made zoos to keep animals in
museums and rural ghettos to keep us away
White people believe we are from the land
and they are from somewhere else
some place *better* than us
I believe they are mistaken

The Greatest Show in Town

An ambulance drives by only the lights flashing
no sound no siren
they stop across the street
something happened
nobody cares
not even the woman being
laid out in the stretcher
the only thing growing here is a growing problem
politicians argue
what to do about it
a solution comes by every four years
the ambulance every day
the drug dealers
the hookers
the poor never leave
we are always here *omnipotent*
without end
we are all powerful
we are forever
social workers come and go
worn-out
beaten down
they leave
we've bested them
burned them out
come cops
COME ALL!
our endurance is unbreakable

we are kings
our crowns shine bright
like the flashing lights of cruisers
around the neighbourhood
See us city
we die
we disappear
we are here
come *out of your corner*
cower before our might
our poverty
will pound you into submission
wrestle you
to tears
you love us
you love our meanness
our meaning
you love it when we control you
your talk is cheap
you don't have the balls
Grit
Gumption
Guts
send in the social workers
send in the cops
send in the clowns
we've been twenty-five rounds
with heroin
crack
and

aftershave
hookers
we're not 9 to 5
we're *twenty-four* hour
send in your politicians
your clergymen
and your orphans
we don't believe them anyways
our bright light shines
shines above all
shines
over
our love is boundless
yours unrequited

They Like It Clean

They like it clean
away condoms
away empty bottles

They like it shiny and new
grass to look like rugs
driveways to look like floors

Don't want no cigarette butts either
they go around counting
the blanks
to prove cancer ain't the problem
to prove they pay their taxes

They don't want no Indians around either
got pig farmers and cops to take care of that

They like it shiny and empty
see through you
like you are not even here
were never here
they like it *terra nullius*

They like it shiny and clean
like Mr. Clean
white
blank
empty

White Girl on the Reservation at Night

You shouldn't be out here at night
White girl
you don't want to learn
life here
This place is guarded by *Windigo*
and street gangs
down *Walk-house Bay*
and up to the sewage treatment plant

Bearwalkers are set for revenge
over some past wrong
you don't wanna be here
here White girl
the rebellion is still *goin on*

Go with the old women
closed up in their shacks
fixing their fish nets
for the dawn

Go with some tea and pouch of tobacco
roll the old women's cigarettes

Go before the bodies rise
and the moon is high
and the dogs roam
in packs

Don't refuse the lard
and scone
My *grandmothers* give you

Go before the night
begins grasping for its breath

Listen to my *grandmothers'* gossip
and their superstitious
Shaaaaa-ehhhhhh

Curl up with quilts
on the couch
White girl
and listen to the layers of darkness
coming over this place

Light Cannot Be Believed

Christians always believe
the end is near
that time
linear
will end
soon
more and more and more
into smaller spaces

They learn how to bend light
they have learned to count
to infinity
they believe God can count

This is proof
they believe
that they
are on the right side

Wrong Answers

When I went to school
I always had the wrong answers
I had the French answers
and the Indian answers
that was what my Ojibwe mother
and French father taught me
there were two answers to everything

How the hell could there be three answers
a White Protestant answer

One day
we were to bring our Bibles to school
the next
I was pulled out of class and slapped
for bringing the wrong Bible

I knew then
that school sucked
and they had no answers

Residential School Archaeology

Where are the bodies?
you ask me
I don't know
they are there
behind the buildings
out in the fields
where the children used to work

There ground is not empty
it wants to puke-out
our children

The bodies are there
beside baptisms
and last rites

Abortions
with small folded hands
in the earth

Eyes closed
Peace be with you

God forgives some
that do not deserve it

There Is a Stone There

There is a stone there
where
John
had eight Indians killed
after the rebellion
this place
a crumbling stone that marks
confederation
eight bodies share one
grave

Wandering Spirit
Walking The Sky
Bad Arrow
Miserable Man
Iron Body
Crooked Leg
Little Bear
Man Without Blood

(Fathers of Confederation)

The soldiers took the Indian children
from the Roman-Catholic
industrial school nearby

To witness the event
the building of a nation

What I Can Remember

I remember the adults drank
Pabst Blue Ribbon then
and Pepsi tasted sweeter then
and the bottles were 15 cents
but you got 5 cents back
for returning the empty

The winters seemed
colder then

The summers seemed
shorter then
and the world was freer then
than it is now

I remember the earth was wilder then
and the people were harder then
than they are now

I remember school was the
worst place in the world then
for a little boy

I remember rivers and bush
and the people around me then
this I will not forget
they have made me what I am now

Living in a Can of Jam

Every Saturday as a child
when I ate breakfast
there was a picture on
the can of jam
a big white house
surrounded by manicured trees
and a lush green lawn

I would stare at it
as I ate
imagined who lived there
probably White people
I thought
White people must live
like this

This was probably like the house
my mother would clean
Big, white, the sun always shining

They stopped making that jam I used to eat
or at least stopped putting it in a can
My mother quit her job and found a better one
I imagined
what White people live like

Christmas Wish Book

I remember the Sears *Christmas Wish Book*
when I was a child
after staring at all the toys
I'd stare at the fridges
the voyeuristic doors open
were always full of pop
I guess they didn't have five kids
a case of pop would barely last a weekend
never any leftovers
and there was never any beer
in the fridge
how strange I thought

Bike

When I was a kid
I remember riding my bike
a 10-speed all over town
my parents were out somewhere past last call
and I would ride after the Saturday night
horror movie
ride
all over town
quiet
dark
cool
I was so cool staying out late
everyone else
asleep
ride down to the beach
empty
streets empty
ride to the mall
nothing
but street lights
and moths
my bike was my road to freedom
magic
the night
quiet
dark
empty

Ocean's Revival

We went to Pentecostal tent revivals
MY MOTHER and me
out on the Island
because MY TEACHERS believed I only
heard half-the-earth
and half-the-ocean
the saints would lay hands on me
covering my ears
so that
I
couldn't
hear
at
all

The power of Jesus
could not stop
the sound of the earth
or the ocean
my mother finally lost faith
and took me to *Sick Children's Hospital*
in Toronto
now only the ocean speaks to me

Where the Gravel Road Ends

I know this gulag
with its neon sign
peddling illegal cigarettes
to White people
for Indians smoking
is a government concession stand
I know its one gas-bar
selling watered-down gas
gulag gas
water you don't have to boil
to drink

This is the place where they found
Minamata - the mercury disease
and stubborn tuberculosis
that refuses to die
like us

The bush always beckoning
gravel road to end

The land God gave to Cain
and us the gulag

Growing Up Highway People

Mr. Findley lived across the gravel road
well it really wasn't a road
it was more like a trailer park
now that I remember it
he gave us apples on Saturday afternoons

Next to him lived old Tilley
with about a hundred cats
she loved cats and hated children
well us at least

And old Ben (everyone older than you is old when
   you're a kid)
he'd get drunk and take out his .22 and shot her cats
after, he'd go over to her trailer with a bottle
of his home-made wine and make love to her
or it was just cats wounded?

One time old Ben passed out with some soup on the
   furnace and his place caught fire
my Dad and Mr. Lundy pulled him out of that inferno
and he moved away
from this hell

Some Indians lived there too
awhile, part of a government program to civilize the
    Indians
I think they got homesick
or just sick of the place
and left

Along the highway
next to the dump
a little yellow school bus would take us thirty miles
down the highway to school
to another hell

When my father found a place in town we moved
    away too
became town people, well not really
highway people could never become
town people, that's *Dante's hell*

Highway people are amputated to all others
and only
connected by distance

Road Kills

When the Whites found gold
in Tsilhqot'in territory
they built roads on the graves

This black pavement
that the Whites put down is built with the skin of Indians
Telloot
Klatsassin
Tah-pitt
Piele
Chessus

Road kills anything in its path
raccoons, bears, skunks, muskrats, coyotes, rabbits, deer
there is no escape

Road hates life
road hates time
rolls out to destroy

Road wants to escape
road has no memory

Road hates trees
road hates earth
road does not understand language
it has its own
a scowl
a scar
road runs it over

Road knows no endings or beginnings
road runs naked

Road knows life
and raw meat

Road has ideas
about killing everything in its path

Outside a Bar in Sioux Lookout

Outside a bar in Sioux Lookout there
is an Indian man
selling his paintings
they will be worth something someday, but not today

Today they are worth
a bottle of wine

Today they are worth
Queen Elizabeth's silver tea set

Today they are worth
the first stone thrown at Mary Magdalene

Today they are worth the night
the angel entered Mary
and Joseph never knew

Today they are worth the night
Marilyn Monroe died

Today they are worth
being baptized in the Jordan river

Tonight they will be worth
a dance with a pretty girl

Commonalities

Smuggle smokes across the border
like Palestinians smuggle theirs
the only difference is New York or Egypt

Entice the White people on to the reserve
with a casino
lead them to their vice
Then they can bitch about the money they lost and taxes

On the way out
go into the White town for grub
stares and questions about
Your breed?

And back home
but instead of *Soweto* homelands
its *Red Pheasant* reserve

We watch the world
from beyond lines on a map
and know
all things come back to this word

Consumption of the Have Not

The rich eat the poor
the poor try not to be eaten
they make pudding from our blood
and boil our fat for vaccines and vacations
to places only ever seen on TV
it is this way

The wealthy
must store the bones of the have not
have not must labour
have not must not weaken
have not makes wealth from
his own flayed flesh
have not have not
cannibals among them

White People and Tanning

I laugh when I see White people tanning themselves
they think it makes them look healthy
it is actually unhealthy to be brown in this country.
The side effects of which are
having to boil your water every time you want a drink
living in mouldy houses
incarceration
illness
colonial sickness
madness
and death slow dying
children

The Longing of Meaning

The daughters become white bitches and old hags
take travel for learning, most of life for granted
and love for refuge

The brothers become old men and dirty old men
work for sanctuary from white bitches and old hags
and lovemaking for broken promises

And the children born to these tides
will watch the slow low suffocation
pretending to know
what only death can follow

Myth of the Land and the People

The only region that matters in this country when it
comes to poetry is Saskatchewan.

Canadians are in love with the idea of the lonesome
prairies, not the place, nobody actually lives there.

Like Newfoundland, or the North. Nobody really lives
in these places or knows what goes on there or really
gives a damn.

Canadians love the idea of empty spaces, an empty
land. Perhaps they believe this because it legitimizes
their claim to it.

Canadians claim that they love the country, the rural
life, but most live in the cities in the south, most hate
nature.

We've cut down the forests, destroyed the east coast
fishery and the west coast fishery. Dammed the rivers
like the country.

The list of extinct animals gets longer, the land is
becoming empty.

Canadians claim they can handle the cold, but most
can't and they escape it moving to Florida and Arizona.
That's really how they handle the cold.

Canadians claim they love the wilderness, but really
most never go there, perhaps only to play Indian for
a weekend or camping.

Canadians love to dream about who they really are,
but who are we really?

We do not know.

Questions White People Have Asked Me

I know a native guy in Winnipeg
You know him?

My great grandmother was Native
Mohawk? I think
Yours?

What breed are you?

Is there a ceremony for seeing a coyote in your yard?

How do we solve the problems of the Natives?
What's your solution?

You mean like, a final solution?

Yeah.

Power

Teachers would write on the wall
in class but we
were not *aloud*
so in the summer
we'd go down
to the school
and smash
the windows
we believed
we would be heard
our power
seen

What White People Know about Indians

What White people know about Indians
can almost fill a post card
from Canada
or a status card
from the government
some of us think of it
as the Star of David
armband
worn by the Jews in Germany
and some of us
try not to think of it
at all

When White People Think about Indians

When White people think about Indians
they think about land
and who owns it
they recall what they've seen at the movies
and twenty-five minutes of history class

When White people think about Indians
they think about how correct their ancestors
were in subjugating the Indian
and how they had nothing to do with it

When Indians think about White people
they have to use their imagination

They have to because there is no such thing
as White people just as there is no such thing as Indians

Three Religious Dogs

The wind is making it minus 30 outside
the dogs just came back
with the weather worn on their beards as icicles

On TV there is a Christian program on
they talk about hope, God and war

The dogs don't pay any attention
they lay at the wood stove
warming their feet

I believe they are Christian

Baawitigong

When the French first arrived at
Sault Ste. Marie
they put up a cross
on a low hill

said some words in French to many Anishnabeg
already gathered there
claiming the land for King Louis XIV of France

as they began to leave
the Indians knocked down the cross

Coureur des Bois, Nomads and Refugees

There is a story in my father's family
that they had some land in Quebec
given to them by the King of France
in a place now called Champlain County
and it was taken away by the King of England

They say they became Coureur des Bois
shortly thereafter
became nomads
lived with Indians
had children
who became refugees

The Française

When Cartier stumbled upon Canada
he stayed the winter
but not by choice

The Marnier lay frozen with hundred of his men

The Indians called them "Carries of the Stick"
and thought them feeble
and feeble-minded

When the Indians met Cartier
he offered them bread and wine
after tasting it the Indians
said of the Frenchmen
"These people drink blood and eat wood"

And indeed they did

and when Cartier left with what was left of his men
in the spring
the Indians were glad to be rid of them

Cannibal Border Economy

The bootlegger's pockets are stuffed full of cash
she loves her money
more than the dealers do
she has more than any cigarette smuggler
but not as much as the gun runners
and not half as much as the casino
and nobody does anything much about it

Entrepreneurs of the dispossessed
businessmen of the poor
merchants of the unsaved
company man of the meagre

Windigo of houses
flesh of mothers
children of nations

Rogue of the infinite fires
this is where the dead rise
zombie whore
resurrecting brown junkies
from their mouldy houses
and gravel alleys

Who will die first?
Who has the money to die here?
Now?

This addiction to twist time
and place into something
recognizable
something that lies between wisps of smoke
and swigs of swill
wicked healer
of the broken

I have your cash
I have your love
bring me my love

The Case against Progress

We spend our time trying to build
something out of nothing
and it always comes to nothing anyway
except a tomb

all that we do disappears
in time
all we say is forgotten
by the world
all that we have touched dies
all we have eaten
is eaten by the earth

we are food for worms
and weeds
here we remain

When You Meet God

When you meet God remind him you are a consumer
tell him you worked your way to the top of the class
and Hollywood made a reality show out of it

Tell him you read all of his flyers
that were dropped off every Saturday
like sacred scrolls
had first row seats to *Jesus Christ Superstar*
and saw *The Ten Commandments* ten times
thought he should have got the Academy
Award for the burning tree bit

Tell him you had no other idols
but a car, a house, a mortgage and Canadian idol
you were against swimming pools
except the one you drowned your sorrows in
and the one you were baptized in

Tell him you have the entire blue-ray collection
of *Twin Peaks* and own not a single Celine Dion song

Tell him you gave money to a homeless man once
to buy wine

Tell him you loved Mc D's and Mc D loved you
that is how you got there

And don't forget to ask him to autograph your Bible

Tangled in a Horn

We will not fly away from here when we die
We will not leave the earth when we die
It is our home
It always has been
It always will be
Always

Jesus will not be coming
Down from space
On a horse
To torture his brother
From underground
And save you from whatever it is you wished to be
    saved from

Allah will not bring you rain
Or mercy
Will not see what you've done or desired

The End will come
Like it came for
The dying
They will not rise
Because you believe
Does not make it so
The wicked go into the ground
The same
The saved

Rest
The dead will not rise
The earth will keep them
This house without light
As it always has
So it is with the world
So it is
What you cannot know
You believe

A Changing of the World

Slave gangs gather
the rain clouds
without peace
or sleep

They gather the rain
with that thunder
that can change worlds

     A
     new
     law

     A
     new
     song

Wake my heart
and drink

What Have They Done to You?

What have they done to you?
What have they made you into?
this thing
meaningless
that meant so much
a corpse of roads
that never find home

What are you now?
a graveyard
for strangers
and their own executioners

The blue house
the yellow birds are gone
an unintelligible noise
an ooze
without form
shapes
of things that were
resemble nothing
that was

What is your noise?
a deprivation
victim of time
architect of change

Believing Will Kill You

Birds believe we don't know how to fly
this they believe until they are eaten by snakes
Fishes believe we don't know how to swim
this they believe until they drown
Snakes believe we don't know how to crawl
this they believe until they are eaten by toads
Toads believe we don't know how to sing
this they believe until they are eaten by fish
Moths believe we don't know moonlight
this they believe until exhausted dead
Men believe in God
this they believe until God kills them

In My House

This is my house
It is mobile
it moves like wind
This is my house:
here we struggle with identity
politics
and strong river currents
I sleep like a baby here
whose mother is out
and does not know it
In my house
the master is the slave
and the slave is the master
In my house
rifles are kept in the closet
My house is built with flesh
and does not search the stars
Here I eat
I sleep
I labour
I live

Part Two

KNOW THIS EARTH

Ways to Talk to the Earth

The land is sacred
there is no getting around this
you are a stranger to it
there is also no getting around this
  my mother braids my hair
  because she loves me

I will tell you something
you do not know
this is the way you talk to the earth
  we listen to the earth
  and it speaks
  seasons
  it sings

My Skin Is Almost the Colour of the Earth

My skin is almost the colour of the earth

My life
flickering
from the embers of a nation

My words are as spider's web
rebuilding
a nation

The red ochre earth
sings to me

Big Bang Drum

This is the big bang
the big bang
bang the drum scatter the universe
the frighten swirl to the women's womb
create the universe
this is the big bang
bang the drum
lay the low yonder

This gale pushes and exhales
stars and suns
bring all round this light
building
circles
this is the drum
that built the universe
dancing a world
from one edge to the end

Bringing down this ending
bring
down
this
ending

Traveller

Travelling up and down this star
a dizzying spin
through a light of this star
a wheel turning
a light
makes you magic
makes you whole
turn again to me
traveller

Word Spaces

Sound rising from your lips
bending the space between us
changing the light
moving the darkness
inhaling time
and beating against my stone drum
singing me again
into a new creation
again and again born
call me again
into your creation
sound painted red
with ochre
rising

There Is Power

She folds this side of the sky
over
she sings a song
while she does this
her warm breath

There is power
her breasts are swollen
for me
ready
make ready

There is power

An Act of Creation

Where men stand in the ocean
they shrivel
women point
this is their power
where ocean speaks
the world will listen
touch
the world will be created

I Turn the Soil

I turn the soil
where my grandmothers
did
I turn nations
I turn generations
the soil sings
a long memory
sings to me
I dig with my hands
the soil drumming
in my hands
in my blood
I can hear the beat
I turn the soil
I turn nations
the soil sings
it says
I turn generations

A Cathedral

Sometimes
at my father's house
at night
when the air was still
you could hear the wolves
singing
they have found God

Imagination of Cows

The cows are eating the spring buds from
an apple tree
they squeeze themselves
against the barb wire fence
flick their tails
against the incessant flies
they squeeze themselves
against the farmers' imagination
and mine too

The mind of men
have never known
what
an apple tree bud
could taste like

What the Rain Makes Possible

I am dancing in your rain
and that makes me beautiful
I dance
I celebrate
with the orchids
lilacs
and tiger lilies
the dew worms dance
and the robins rejoice

We celebrate
wet
we dance
this rain

Early Morning

When you woke me
with the mountains rushing down
the memory of gravity
is infinite
sleep is a wound to your beauty
a curse to your body
wake me before
the night stretching out to the
remnants of a dream
its bony fingers clutching
my mysteries rise
with the moon and the tides
woman oh
women
heart of the earth
lift my tongue from
its silence

Vanishing a Universe

You are far away now
a universe
travelled
summer breath no-longer against our
bodies
love is rare
and winter will bury all memory
and will not answer these last
kisses
this kindness will be
forgotten
this corpse

Maniacal Lover of Delilah

I am not your Samson
after the wine glass
after you've cut my hair
I will not be still
your Samson
I will follow you
into the Philistine camp
I will raise the sun
and tie my sleep around you
I will follow you
I will crush my temple
and my vows
till I can see Gaza
no more

Exposing Aphrodite

You are like an ocean
slashing at the pier
beckoning fisherman to fear
sleepless
they come to you

Lay still
they whisper
we want to love you

Scatter my nets
deep to your heart
cradle my boat
in your killer hands

Kiss me with your
frozen breath

Take us in
your mouth
and show us how
Aphrodite was born

Nature Will Have Order

There were cats here one time
Black & White, Big Orange, Winky (because she only
   had one eye)
they lived in the shed across the driveway
near the barn
fed on mice and birds and whatever else they could
   catch
they went in heat
and *Big Orange* would scrap over near the barn
whatever strange cat came along
he must have won
because most of the kittens looked like him
then they began to die
because nature has its own
eugenics laws

There are no cats here now
there are only birds
because nature needs order
before anything else

Aboriginal Women

Indian women don't take crap
they lie with lilies and wake up
smelling like earth
their laughter is clear
and has healing
for the soul

Native women don't take crap
they can make you whole
and keep you warm
your heart still wild
like *Lake Superior copper*
and kisses like sunlight
pressed onto your lips
Indian women don't take crap
at least not in love

Farmer Home

The men are brut
and blind to that natural light
they are guided to the seasons
by the sound of geese
parting or
returning
guided by the cold and
the feel of leaves falling
they are guided by
love, laughter
and the sound
of tractors in golden fields
grasping what the earth
grows
they are blind to that natural light
that darkens forearms
and faces
makes leather
that grows every morning
and dies every night
that water can't defeat
but does
the light that follows home footsteps
for them
that light on small faces
for them
there is nothing more natural

Boiled Moose Nose Soup

First
kill a moose
cut off his noose
and all other edible parts
build a fire
skewer the nose
and pass it in to the fire
one-two-three
that's enough!
take a knife
scrape off the hair
and cut nose into bite-sized pieces
add onions
salt
pepper (if handy)
simmer
till tender
eat
smell like a moose

Twisting Smokes in Rural Ghetto

Women fix their sorrowful gardens
the bush creeping to the carrots and the
proud onions

Men head out to scatter and gather fishing nets
hoping they will not return the same

Only the light changes

Split wood for the coming cold
buy bullets for the coming colours

Fading

Have tea and sew birch-bark baskets
for visitors from other ghettos
twist smokes
in wrinkled brown hands
that have snatched flopping fish
from the bottom of the boat
smoke
only the light
orders this world

Chant the Circle

This land is my homeland
the wind chant
the water chant
the ground chant
me into being

I am born
chant
sing back to them
briefly
I pass
away

I begin
chant

Turn This Way

Turn this way to me
and do not forget
the fury of this land
this land
raw beauty
the lashes of winter
the kiss of spring
turn this way to me
I will show you summer rising
from plumes of snow
I will show you
an angry Autumn
and deep burrows of memory
all the rancid seasons
this land I will show you
turn this way to me

A Partridge Answers

Everybody knows birds can't
read the poetry of Rilke
stupid bird

I understand the structure
of the Birch and the Ash
can hear the Maple leaves
falling in the Beaver's pond

I know the stanza of pebbles
the songs of powdered snow
I call out to love
and it comes to me

I know the sweetness of spring
and remember God

I know the true name of him

I know where the wind goes

I witness life

I am my being

Pets

My sister had two rabbits
Xiomara and Wilbur
they were kept in the backyard
elaborate cage
her boyfriend built for them

One winter night
they froze to death
I found them early next morning
and brought them in

My sister skinned and cleaned them
because we didn't know what else
to do with them
we ate them
rabbit stew

They were pets
but they were also animals
brought the skins to my grandmother
and I think
my sister still has the mitts

My Garden

I wait here in the garden
to watch the flowers wilt
away with the light

The hummingbirds to eat
lick the last of the nectar

Slugs make their way in
follow the flowers
frogs follow them

Beetles tumble up the earth
digging their way to their desires

The light lifts everything here
and I wait to be lifted

Epistle of the River

The river doesn't slow here
even in winter people sit beside it
and watch the water burrow itself into the rock

The river curls itself around this massif
it sings to the boulders
sings to the earth

The undercurrents beckoning
What wrestles in the currents?
What drowns in the boiling water?

This song without end

The stones are silent

Philosophy of Fireflies

They spoke to stones like
they were speaking to the dead
only when they shined
sang to the earth
with vapours
and motion
       What is it to be human?
Inside
Song
Shivers
       What is it to the living?
Only
Fireflies
Can
Know

Only they count
the stars
only they know the number

Melody with Light

Fireflies make melody
with light
memory flashes of summer

Sparks of love
naked tips of sun
glimmers of love

Night gnaws the light away

A Father to His Son

When you feel hatred remember love
When you feel ignorant remember understanding
When you feel caged remember freedom
When you feel like dying remember living
When you feel like crying remember laughter
When you feel like fighting remember peace
When you feel like letting go remember to hold on
When you feel dark remember *your light*
When you feel like cursing remember praying
When you feel like shouting remember to whisper
When you feel like going blind remember the beauty
    inside you
When you feel ungrateful remember to be thankful
When you feel the night will not end remember the
    morning will come
When you feel like lying down remember to stand up
When you feel like no one remember *you are someone*
When you feel pride remember humility
When you feel like winter remember spring
When you feel ungodly remember God *is in you*
And when you feel unloved remember I love you
    always

I Live in the Borderlands

This borderland ghost dance
I am twenty people
I know
Where the drum was buried
Before the white man came
I know hate
But I do not remember it
I remember time before white people
Unearth the drum *Earth*!
I know what you cannot believe
I am twenty people
Know this earth
Know me
Like this earth knows me

Notes

1. *Telloot, Klatsassin, Tah-pitt, Piele, Chessus, Tsilhqot'in* are Indians executed by Judge Matthew Begbie in 1864 in the aftermath of what is known as the Chilcotin war.

2. *Wandering Spirit, Walking The Sky, Bad Arrow, Miserable Man, Iron Body, Crooked Leg, Little Bear, Man Without Blood* are Cree Indians executed in 1885 during the largest mass execution in Canadian history.

3. *Terra nullius* is a Latin expression meaning *Belonging to no one* or *No man's land.*

4. *Baawitigong* is Ojibwa for *Place of the rapids.*

5. *Anishnabeg* is Ojibwa for *Original People.*

6. *Windigo* is Ojibwa for *Cannibalistic monster.*